Dispatches From The MGT.

Curious Signs from the American Workplace

Compiled by Steve Johnson

Brainfart Press, Barlow, KY
www.brainfartpress.com

This book is dedicated to
Markoff Chaney
A little man with big balls

Dispatches From The MGT.

Curious Signs from the American Workplace

Management. Every company has it, and in some companies the managers seem to outnumber the employees, but most people aren't really sure why it exists. Middle management in particular provides no apparent value to the company. In fact, they usually just get in the way. Why are they there? What are they getting paid to do? When will they leave us alone?

In my time in the workplace, I've only been able to determine one specific thing that managers do: They make signs. The value of these signs to the continued operation and profitability of the company, much like the value of management itself, is unclear, but the signs themselves can be fascinating. Sometimes they're incomprehensibly bizarre, sometimes they provide insight into the almost alien attitudes that management has towards the rank-and-file employees, and sometimes they're unintentionally hilarious.

While signs will never completely disappear from the workplace, the rapid adoption of email, text messaging, and other forms of electronic communication in nearly all industries has reduced the prominence of signs in the workplace. I've compiled this book as a way to preserve some of the greatest examples of what may be called the Golden Age of Workplace Signs, which started in the 1980s and ended around the turn of the century. I present these signs with no commentary other than a notation of where they were found. Interpreting what they say about the American psyche, capitalism, the Dunning-Kruger Effect, or anything else is beyond my expertise. This book is simply meant to showcase a dying and often unrecognized art form.

Found at:
Chemical Plant,
Hoboken, New Jersey

DO NOT
Rock Out
with your
Cock Out
until you
Clock Out

--MGT.

Found at:
Hardware Supply Warehouse,
Boise, Idaho

Never Lift With Your Back

Always Lift With Your
Heart

Found at:
Adult Novelty Store
Lawrence, Kansas

Remember:

If

YOU

Let The Customers Down

They'll Kill Themselves

--MGT.

Found at:
Machine Shop
Dryden, Ohio

PLEASE
DO NOT
CHEW GUM
OR LEATHER
ON THE SHOP
FLOOR

MGT.

Found at:
Marketing Firm
New York, New York

Mandatory Meeting
MONDAY
3:15 pm

We will discuss the recent issues we've had with tardiness and crippling existential despair

-MGT.

Found at:
Call Center
Collinsville, Illinois

Please remember that the manager's office overlooks the cubicles.

We can see you masturbating, Phil.

--MGT.

Found at:
Clothing Store
Birmingham, Alabama

PLEASE
DO NOT
SHIT HERE

~MGT.

Found at:
Tech Firm
Seattle, Washington

Your Restroom
Visit May Be
Monitored For
Quality Control
Purposes

--MGT.

Found at:
Sceince Museum
Tampa, Florida

Please do not tell members of the press to "eat shit and die in a fire."

--MGT.

Found at:
Cab Company
Des Moines, Iowa

Cindy is selling candy bars to pay for uniforms for her son's baseball team. You can purchase them from either Cindy or the dispatcher, but they taste like shit.

Found at:
Chinese Buffet
Scranton, Pennsylvania

Limit
1 Chopstick
Per Customer

Found at:
Food Co-Op
Portland, Oregon

All Interviews Must Be Conducted Skyclad

--MGT.

Failure to clock in will result in summary execution

--MGT.

SEXUAL HARASSMENT WILL NOT BE TOLERATED

Except by Ethel in Accounting.
That Old Lady is DTF.

-MGT.

Found at:
National Hamburger Chain
Las Vegas, Nevada

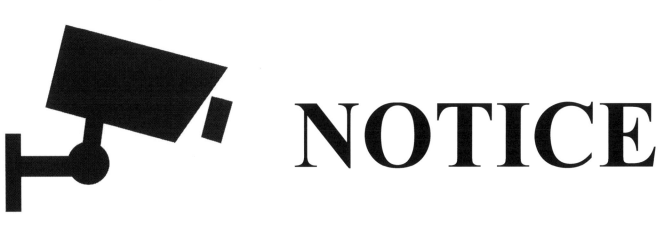 NOTICE

Ketchup Dispenser
Monitored
At All Times

--MGT.

Found at:
Accounting Firm
Jacksonville, Florida

Secret Santa Gifts Should Not Be Over $20 or Used Sex Toys

--MGT.

Found at:
Restaurant Decorations Warehouse
Possum Trot, Kentucky

As of November
1st the company
insurance plan will no
longer cover dental,
vision, handjobs, or
prescription shoes.

--MGT.

Found at:
Barber Shop
Beaver, Utah

No Smoking in Employee Restroom Except After Sex

--MGT.

Found at:
Bottling Plant
Trout, Idaho

All Visitors Must Have Appointment And Bring Gift

--MGT.

Found at:
Call Center
Collinsville, Illinois

REMINDER:
Anyone Who Doesn't Go To Phil's Fucking Improv Show This Weekend Will Probably Never Hear The End Of It

--MGT.

Found at:
Retail Pottery Store
Bangor, Maine

If a customer with a John Deere cap and a rebel flag tattoo tells you he needs to show you something, say NO.

It's his penis.

--MGT.

Found at:
Airport
St. Louis, Missouri

REMINDER:

It's "A" Dildo
NOT
"Your" Dildo

--MGT.

Found at:
Retail Chain Headquarters
Bentonville, Arkansas

Occult Rituals are not to be conducted during work hours without prior approval from diversity office.

Found at:
Telemarketing Firm
Detroit, Michigan

It's Hard To Soar
With The Eagles
When You're
Surrounded By
Vile Incompetent
Fuckstains.

Found at:
Self-Storage Facility
Beaver, Utah

PLEASE DO NOT USE AS STRIPPER POLE

--MGT

Found at:
Auto Parts Store
Tempe, Arizona

Please do
not write or
draw penises
on walls,
fixtures, or
merchandise.

--MGT.

Found at:
Chicken Processing Plant
Peoria, Illinois

In response to numerous requests placed in the suggestion box, the 3rd shift supervisor will eat shit and die during shift change on Friday.

--MGT.

Shoplifters Will Be Prosecuted. Hipsters Will Be Persecuted.

--MGT.

Found at:
Science Museum
Tampa, Florida

Please do not refer to the customers as "A bunch of filthy, uneducated cocksuckers" when speaking with the press.

--MGT.

Found at:
Marketing Firm
Louisville, Kentucky

Please stop demanding that the new IT guy give you a pot of gold. He is not a leprechaun.

--MGT.

Found at:
Coffee Shop
Shreveport, Louisiana

All Employees
Must Wash Hands
and Taint Before
Returning To
Work

Found at:
Shopping Mall
Bakersfield, California

Please Do Not Throw Coins Or Feces Into Fountain

MGT.

Found at:
Call Center
Collinsville, Illinois

If whoever took Phil's Fleshlight returns it to the break room by close of business tomorrow, there will be no questions asked.

--MGT.

Found at:
Bank Headquarters
Wilmington, North Carolina

On Monday we will be taking up donations to help the Vice President of Marketing buy a new boat. The one he currently has is only a 40-footer and some of the guys at the club make fun of him. Please give if you can. Anyone who contributes more than $500 will be allowed to dress "casual" from 3:30-5 on Friday.

Thanks,
MGT.

Found at:
Magazine Publisher
Indianapolis, Indiana

When referring to Holly's religious beliefs, the preferred terminology is "Pagan" or "Wiccan." "Flaky New Age Nonsense" is unacceptable.

Found at:
Law Firm
Boston, Massachusetts

If anyone knows a good place to get some weed, please contact Ethel in Accounting.

Found at:
Comic Book Store
Concord, New Hampshire

Please do not tell the customers about all the cool shit we keep in the back room but won't sell them.

Found at:
Mass Market Retail Store
Wheeling, West Virginia

Remember, "Union" is just one letter away from "Onion," and onions make you cry!

Found at:
Computer Supply Warehouse
Atlanta, Georgia

Once again: the bar code scanners are NOT to be used for playing laser tag.

--MGT.

Found at:
Chain Book Store
Columbus, Ohio

Please Do Not Try To Convince Co-Workers That You Are A Time-Traveler From The Future.

Found at:
IT Company
Springfield, Missouri

Our offices will be closed on March 19 in observance of Client's Day

Found at:
Diner
Phoenix, Arizona

All Side Work Should Be Done Off The Clock.

Found at:
Construction Site
Omaha, Nebraska

Hard Hats & Pants Required In This Area At All Times

Found at:
Call Center
Collinsville, Illinois

Please refrain from staring at, openly discussing, or asking questions about Phil's new prosthesis. He's very self-conscious about it.

--MGT.

Found at:
Science Museum
Tampa, Florida

Please refrain from telling members of the media that the company is "run by Satan-Worshipping Pigfuckers."

--MGT.

Found at:
Injection Molding Facility
Boise, Idaho

If a co-worker gets pulled into the grinder, please stop what you are doing and clean all blood and viscera from blades before loading any new material into the machine. An incident report should be filed at the end of the shift.

Found at:
Car Dealership
Gallup, New Mexico

On Friday, the office manager will be giving a presentation in order to demonstrate that he does, in fact, know his own ass from a hole in the ground.

Attendance is mandatory.

--MGT.

Found at:
Investment Bank
New York, New York

There shall come a culling at the end of next quarter. All employees with low performance review scores will be sacrificed to the Dark Lord.

Found at:
Call Center
Collinsville, Illinois

We appreciate everyone's efforts to save money and protect the environment, but please remember to use the backs of photocopies of genitals for internal documents only.

--MGT.

Found at:
Payroll Services Company
Denver, Colorado

Remember that failing to report a fellow employee for stealing office supplies is not that different from genocide.

Found at:
Medical Billing Office
Rapid City, South Dakota

"Casual Friday" does not mean "Clothing Optional Friday."

--MGT.

Janet has requested that rather than throw her a baby shower, we take up a collection so she can get an abortion. If you'd like to contribute, please contact Sally.

Found at:
Web Services Firm
Renton, Washington

Due to low sales numbers this quarter, there will be a freeze on all raises for the remainder of the fiscal year. The CFO will be flying in on the new company jet next Thursday to answer any questions you may have.

MGT.

Effective immediately, all press inquires should be referred to the Public Relations Department.

--MGT.

Found at:
Package Delivery Hub
Knoxville, Tennessee

Break Time Belongs To You. Work Time Belongs to Nyarlathotep

If an employee faints from heat exhaustion, the employee who finds them is responsible for completing their order.

--MGT.

Found at:
Seafood Restaurant
Brooklyn, New York

An automatic gratuity of 15% will be added to the bill of parties who look like assholes.

Found at:
Greeting Card Store
Oklahoma City, Oklahoma

Employees are not allowed to panhandle during work hours

--MGT.

Found at:
Self-Storage Facility
Green Bay, Wisconsin

This Area Is Being Monitored By A Maladjusted Pervert

Found at:
Call Center
Collinsville, Illinois

There Will Be Cake To Celebrate Mike's Birthday During Afternoon Break on Thursday. It's Also Phil's Birthday, But Fuck That Guy. --MGT.